LITURGY AND DOCTRINE

CHARLES DAVIS

Liturgy and Doctrine

The Doctrinal Basis of the Liturgical Movement

SHEED AND WARD
LONDON AND MELBOURNE

FIRST PUBLISHED 1960
SHEED AND WARD LTD
33 MAIDEN LANE
LONDON W.C.2
AND
SHEED AND WARD PTY LTD
28 BOURKE STREET
MELBOURNE

FIFTH IMPRESSION 1966

NIHIL OBSTAT: JOANNES M. T. BARTON, S.T.D., L.S.S.
CENSOR DEPUTATUS

IMPRIMATUR: ✠ GEORGIUS L. CRAVEN, VIC. GEN.
EPUS SEBASTOPOLIS

WESTMONASTERII, DIE 13A AUGUSTI, 1960

The *Nihil Obstat* and *Imprimatur* are a declaration that a book
or pamphlet is considered free from doctrinal or moral error.
It is not implied that those who have granted the *Nihil Obstat*
and *Imprimatur* agree with the contents, opinions or statements
expressed.

This book is set in 11 on 12 Linotype Baskerville

Made and printed in Great Britain by
William Clowes and Sons, Limited, London and Beccles

CONTENTS

		Page
1.	THE CHARACTER OF THE LITURGICAL MOVEMENT	9
2.	THE RISEN CHRIST . . .	20
3.	THE HISTORY OF SALVATION . .	36
4.	THE CHURCH	47
5.	LITURGY AND MYSTERY . . .	60
6.	SACRIFICE AND SACRAMENTS . .	75
7.	ESCHATOLOGY	91
8.	CONCLUSION	98

ACKNOWLEDGEMENT

THIS essay develops at greater length ideas that were briefly outlined in an article in *The Clergy Review*, November 1959. We are indebted to the Editor and The Tablet Publishing Co., Ltd., for permission to make use of matter from that article.

1

THE CHARACTER OF THE LITURGICAL MOVEMENT

I T is paradox to say it of so great a mystery, but essentially the liturgy is an ordinary affair for Christians. It forms the centre of the ordinary life of the Church. At its basic and most vital it simply means that Christians gather together and meet one another and carry out together, each according to his place in the Church, the normal and distinctive activities that belong to them as Christians. There is nothing esoteric or exclusive or optional about the liturgy; it is part and parcel of the Christian life.

This simple truth should govern our practical attitude to the liturgy. No doubt it is a great mystery, as is everything that flows from Christ and brings us into Christ; but, since it is something where the average run of Christians have their part to play, it inevitably involves a virile ordinariness on its human side. After all, a family meal is often a ragged affair, with the baby hammering on the table and adolescent voices sounding raucous and uncouth, but it would be an odd situation, and one in which the true values of the occasion would be submerged, if the members were compelled to silence while a well-

trained voice read poetry to them. The Mass
is the family meal of the Christian community.
By all means let there be as much dignity and
beauty as possible—a lively sense of the sacred
must never be absent—but it is better for things
to be carried out in an externally untidy way with
everyone taking a real part, than to have a fault-
less performance with the congregation looking
on passively. The church is not a theatre but a
house. It is a family that is gathered together,
not an audience. The people are there to take
part, not to watch.

We should banish without reprieve any idea
that the liturgy is a private hobby, of interest to
some but not to others. It is not the preserve
of those who have a liking for ceremonies. To
be liturgically minded has nothing to do with
aestheticism or affected refinement. With the
liturgy we are dealing with the ordinary, every-
day life of the present-day Church. Unless we
turn from the subject of ancient chasubles and
grapple with the raw material of the Christian
community as it is here and now with its needs
and capabilities, we remain in the field of antiquarian studies and outside that of liturgy.

The liturgy is at the centre of the pastoral
work of the Church. Interest in the liturgy and
study of the liturgy mean interest in the pastoral
work of the Church and study of it. That is the
angle from which to approach the liturgy and
concern ourselves with it. And we have the wit-
ness of history to support this contention. A long
and complicated evolution lies behind the present

shape of our liturgy. Was there any directive principle? Is there any key factor that explains the creation of new liturgical forms and the many changes in liturgical rites? Historical studies provide a clear answer. The inner direct-ing force of liturgical development through the centuries has been the pastoral concern of the Church and its unceasing endeavour to fulfil its pastoral charge in the liturgy.

The same factor is the mainspring of the pre-sent liturgical movement and alone explains it. That is why it is not an awakening of interest in certain features of ancient ritual, a movement akin to, say, the Gothic revival. It is a down-to-earth pastoral movement, working for the renewal of the Christian life of ordinary people at its centre and source.

At least, it is now. There have been two or even three phases in the modern liturgical movement. The first phase belongs to the nine-teenth century. It was dominated by Guéranger, the founder of Solesmes. His work has come in for some very heavy criticism in recent years. The criticism has erred by excess. Some of his ideas are plainly unacceptable, but it would be wrong to dismiss this first stage of the movement as merely aesthetic and antiquarian. It would be more accurate to call it monastic. Guéranger tried to spread abroad the doctrinal and devo-tional riches of the liturgy; he wanted to make the prayer of the Church the basis of the per-sonal piety of Christians; and he met with con-siderable success. But the effort remained remote from the ordinary life of the average parish, and too much stress was laid on the external splendour of the liturgy as ideally executed. This remoteness from the ordinary Christian community in its normal functioning led in some quarters to a romantic concern with beautiful inessentials and a failure to bring into sufficient prominence the basic values of the liturgy.

In contrast to this, a strongly pastoral concern marks the second stage in the movement. The forerunner here was undoubtedly St. Pius X, with his restoration of frequent Communion and his attempts to get congregations to sing. His remark designating active participation in the liturgy as the primary and indispensable source of the true Christian spirit is deservedly famous and can serve as the motto of the movement. Nevertheless, papal decrees do not constitute a movement, and for the beginning of the movement properly so called we must turn to Belgium and the work of Dom Lambert Beauduin. The remark of Pius X just mentioned was made in *Tra le Sollecitudini* of 1903. It was a few years later, at the Catholic Congress of Malines in 1909, that Dom Lambert put forward his programme. We have just celebrated the fiftieth anniversary of that congress, where many would place the birth of the movement in its present form. From then onwards there grew in Belgium a popular pastoral movement aiming at a renewal of the Christian life of ordinary people through the liturgy as its primary source. Dom Lambert's booklet *La Piété de l'Eglise*, first published in 1914, sums up its principles and aims and is still well worth reading. The Belgian movement introduced and promoted the use of the dialogue Mass and brought about the widespread use of vernacular missals by the faithful.

The liturgical movement would not, however, be what it is at present without what took place in Germany. We may take as the starting-point of the German movement the méeting of a new society of Catholic laymen—university teachers, doctors and lawyers—which took place at Maria Laach in the Holy Week of 1914. They met to discuss ways and means of promoting the more active share of the faithful in the Mass. The pioneer here was Ildefons Herwegen, who had been made the Abbot of Maria Laach in the previous year. His first concern had not been with an outside apostolate but with the communal life of his own monastery. He strove to give it a greater unity than before. This was done by making the liturgy the centre of all the activity of the monastery, intellectual, practical and religious. The domestic achievement had wide repercussions. The strong and unified community life, with its marked liturgical bias, gave the monastery an unsurpassed influence on those who came into contact with it. A full account of the German movement would have to mention other personalities and centres, but we are not wrong in giving the decisive role to Maria Laach as led by Abbot Herwegen.

The liturgical movement that developed between the wars in Germany has been, and still is, of such power that it will be seen in history as a determining and formative force in the modern Church. Although at first decidedly less popular and less realistic in approach than its counterpart in Belgium, it soon came to grips with the realities of ordinary parochial existence. But where it became most outstanding was in the quality of its liturgical scholarship and the depth of its doctrinal reflection. In this respect, we immediately think of the work of Dom Odo Casel, monk of Maria Laach. Whatever hesitations may have been felt about the "theology of mysteries" in the precise form in which he expounded it, few would deny now that his work has served to uncover the doctrinal richness implicit in the liturgy in a way that has transformed the theology of the sacraments, and of the Eucharist in particular. Nor must we forget the scriptural and patristic emphasis given to the movement in Germany and Austria. The latter country saw the great popular apostolate of Pius Parsch, with its strongly biblical character. In brief, there emerged in Germany one of the most influential movements yet seen in the history of the Church, a vast movement of pastoral renewal, but with the pastoral effort backed and directed by scriptural, patristic and doctrinal learning and reflection rarely surpassed. It is well to remind ourselves that, although the restoration of the Paschal Vigil came as a bolt from the blue to us, it had been prepared and made possible on the historical, doctrinal and pastoral levels by the work done in Germany.

The mention of the restoration of the Paschal Vigil leads us to consider the third stage of the liturgical movement. This is really only the continuation of the second stage and is not sharply distinct from it, as the second stage was from the first. It is the stage of liturgical reform. What happened was that the historical, doctrinal and pastoral work brought the realization that our present liturgy was not in a healthy state. Historical studies laid bare the evolution of the liturgy and showed the reasons why the liturgy had ceased to play the part in the ordinary Christian life that it should. One conclusion became clear: if vitality was to be restored to the liturgical life of the Church, changes must be made. Historical studies made it possible to discern which changes would be foreign to the liturgy and due to some unfounded modern fashion. There was no question of a mere desire to restore ancient liturgical practice. The aim was to uncover the liturgical tradition of the Church and gain an insight into its nature and content. The process is a familiar one in theology. A doctrine is renewed by reflection on the past tradition of the Church and by reaching beyond more recent formulations. A striking example of this is the modern renewal in our understanding of the Church. Owing to the need to combat various errors, attention was concentrated for centuries on the Church as a visible and hierarchical society. This one-sidedness has been overcome by going back to the earlier tradition and digging out the rich data found there on the other aspects of the Church. It is the same with liturgical renewal: a return to tradition to overcome the defects of the present. Pastoral necessity shows the need for reform. Historical study, doctrinal reflection and pastoral experience, all help to determine its direction. It was in that way that the new order of Holy Week was achieved—an order which is both ancient and new, a restoration yet one adapted to present pastoral needs.

Prominence has been given to the work done in Germany, and this simply corresponds to the facts. But the French also deserve a mention. True, France did not really get going with regard to a pastoral liturgical movement until towards the end of the Second World War. When she did, however, her contribution proved invaluable. The French produced a flood of clear and reasonably popular writing on the subject. Not all was gold, and there was some dross. There was in some quarters a too hasty adaptation of the liturgy to the requirements of the apostolate. This was a mistake. Liturgy cannot be created; it must be received. It is a traditional datum, which we must accept and make our own. But we can well overlook any early fumbling when we think how much the movement in other countries owes to the skill and energy with which the French expounded the relevant ideas. And where the French have been outstanding is in the biblical movement, so closely and vitally connected with any true understanding of the liturgy. They have been foremost in responding to *Divino*

Afflante Spiritu and incorporating the results of biblical criticism into Catholic thought. More important, they have pursued the work of the doctrinal understanding of the Bible—the work, that is, of biblical theology. The *Bible de Jérusalem* is a landmark, both in restoring the Bible as a living element in the thought and piety of the faithful and in presenting a Catholic understanding of it that is both critical and theological.

The movement in English-speaking countries has been largely derivative. When we take stock of our situation in the light of what is being achieved elsewhere, we cannot but notice the superficial character of so much of our apostolic effort. Where lies our weakness? We refuse to acknowledge the power of ideas. We neglect the content of what we preach. We are anxious to devise ways and means of getting an ever-bigger audience to hear what we say but we will not devote the time, effort and discussion necessary to improve the quality of what we say. So often it is taken for granted that we are already in full possession of what we have to get across, that our possession of it is perfect, stable and nicely balanced, so that all we have to do is to work out ways and means of getting it across. It never seems to occur to us that people sometimes do not listen, because what we tell them is not worth their attention and does not meet their legitimate needs and desires.

The inadequacy found in so many current popular accounts of Catholic teaching is the inadequacy of the out-of-date. It is being overcome in the Church by various forces of doctrinal renewal, among which the liturgical movement is prominent. A considerable obstacle to these forces is a widespread complacency that ignores the inadequacy and presumes, quite wrongly, that because the Catholic faith does not change, our possession and account of it can never be improved. Many must have heard the cry that went up for a kerygmatic theology. Rightly understood, this is not a new branch of theology but an attempt to bring the work of theology into closer touch with what is required for the proclamation and teaching of the Christian message or *kerygma*. What lies behind this striving for a new approach in theology is the conviction that methods in preaching and teaching are not enough; our concern must be principally with the content and structure of our message. Our complacency, then, must be shattered; we must realize that all is not well in this matter. The literature already available is not fully used because of a failure to take to heart the need for serious doctrinal reflection and improvement.

And the need today to improve the content and structure of our message is urgent. The decisive factor in the present critical phase in the history of the Church does not lie in organization and multifarious activities but in a renewal of the religious consciousness of Christian people. Priests must work to deepen in the faithful the awareness of the great truths of our faith and improve the quality of belief. We should be acting like ostriches, were we to ignore the inferior quality of belief in so many of our people. They have little hold upon truths that are central to the Christian message and cling to what is peripheral. Often they have been given but a lopsided and impoverished presentation of Christian truth. What is going on at the present time is a great rethinking of the content of our faith. The liturgical, biblical and catechetical revivals are busy, not simply with practical matters, but with a doctrinal renewal. That is the source of their strength and a guarantee of their enduring influence.

How, then, shall we describe the character of the liturgical movement? It is a movement of pastoral renewal, intimately connected with the biblical and catechetical revivals. It is based on a work of doctrinal reflection that is having repercussions on most parts of Catholic doctrine and theology. It is supported by an historical scholarship of the highest quality, in no way lacking in critical rigour. A general renewal of the life of the Church, it is a *liturgical* movement because the liturgy is at the centre of the life and pastoral work of the Church.

Our concern here is with the doctrinal renewal which it has brought and which underlies its more practical efforts.

2

THE RISEN CHRIST

By now almost everyone has heard the word "Christocentric". There is a general recognition that our preaching, teaching and theology must be Christocentric. The *kerygma* or message is centred on Christ, and we should respect that structure. The universal acknowledgement of this is a great step forward, but the matter goes deeper than is often thought. What has not as yet its central place in the Christian consciousness of Catholics is the risen humanity of Christ. How do most of the faithful think of Christ? When they think of him as man, they think of him as an historical figure. They have in mind Jesus as he lived in Palestine, teaching and working miracles and then dying for us on the Cross. When they think of him as he is at present, when they pray to him, they think of him almost always as God. This does not mean that they would countenance for one moment the idea that Jesus has ceased to be man, nor is it denied that they see him imaginatively as man. But what alone is important for them is his godhead. Jesus is God, the God we worship—that is all they are aware of. What is lacking is the awareness of the risen Christ as the *mediator* through whom we have access to the

Father; an awareness of Christ who by his resurrection has become in his *humanity* life-giving. It is Jesus the man who has been exalted as the source of life for us, so that our Christian life is a share in his risen life.

We go to God the Father in and through Christ; that is, in and through the glorified humanity of Christ. The structure of liturgical prayer indicates this: *"Per Dominum nostrum Jesum Christum."* How foreign that structure is to the personal piety of Catholics! Yet how can we enter into the Eucharist and take part in it unless we make that structure our own? In the Mass we have to enter into Christ's surrender of himself to his Father and worship God the Father through and in Christ. In Holy Communion we are nourished on the body and blood of the living and glorified Christ and joined to his life-giving humanity. Too many Catholics still see in the Eucharist simply the real presence of a divine person to be adored. The question "Who is present in the Eucharist?" often meets with the answer, "God"—an answer which empties the Eucharist of its proper and immediate content.

The liturgical revival aims at restoring a realization of the risen Christ as our mediator and, as a consequence of this, an intelligent grasp of the structure of liturgical prayer and sacrifice: *"Per Christum ad Patrem."* Only in this way will participation in the liturgy be properly understood. Such an approach to Christ is as old as Christianity. The early Christian confession

"Jesus is the Lord" expresses the fact that Christ
has been exalted to the right hand of the Father
and, as glorified, now continues to make inter-
cession for men. It is an expression of belief in
the ever-living Christ and in his present activity.
It includes a recognition of his divinity, but of
that divinity as embodied in the glorified man
Jesus, through whom we go to the Father.

Our grasp of all this depends on our understanding of the Resurrection as a mystery of
salvation. For too long Catholic theology considered the Resurrection exclusively from an
apologetic angle and lost sight of it as a mystery
of our faith—indeed, as the centre of the Christian message of salvation; for the *kerygma* is the
proclamation of the paschal mystery. And this
exclusively apologetic approach is still found in
many otherwise admirable books. The Resurrection is seen as the greatest of Christ's miracles,
the most striking proof of his divine mission, but
its meaning as the accomplishment of salvation
is neglected. The restoration of this mystery to
its place has been achieved by the advance of biblical theology. Any recent book on the theology
of Paul or John will make clear the key position
of the Resurrection in the biblical understanding
of the Redemption. Much remains, however,
to be done before these rich findings of biblical
theology are incorporated into the treatise on
the Redemption at a speculative level.

While the biblical scholars were forging ahead
in their rediscovery of the biblical teaching on
Redemption, liturgical scholars were making

clear the fundamental place of the Resurrection in the liturgy—a place manifested in the position of Easter as the centre of the Church's year. Easter is not simply one feast among many; it is *the* feast, the climax of the year, the centre on which all converges. Its place is not a matter of chance or of historical accident but is due to a doctrinal reason: the place of the paschal mystery in the Christian message. The realization of this made intolerable what had happened to the Easter Vigil—the culminating celebration of the entire year carried out in the early morning of Holy Saturday before a handful of loyal but uncomprehending devout. In the consciousness of the Western Church, Easter, in fact, has lost its central place and importance. This fading of Easter into the background must be one of the most significant facts in the history of the Christian life; it was fraught with consequences. The more one realizes the place of Easter, the more astounding does it become. Certainly, an almost frightening example of the ebb and flow possible in the life of the Church and in its understanding of the Faith. The restoration of the Easter Vigil is an achievement of the liturgical movement that must be termed momentous. It will be long before it bears its full fruit; its repercussions will probably extend over centuries. Nothing short of an upheaval is required in the outlook of the average Catholic before it can be properly appreciated. We have hardly begun to achieve this. How many Catholics, when asked what was the greatest feast of the year,

would answer at once and without hesitation,
"Christmas"? And in answering thus, they would
be thinking mainly of the human side of the
birth of Christ. So many of our faithful have but
the dimmest insight into the Christian message
in its central content, because the paschal mystery has not its proper place in their religious
consciousness.

But such criticism is barren by itself. It is
more fruitful to examine the remedy than to
deplore the deficiency. If they are to be properly
appreciated, the fresh ideas touched upon require
closer attention. They give rise to two inseparable
questions: How should we conceive the role of
Christ? And what is the structure of the Christian life as this emerges from reflection on the
liturgy and liturgical prayer?

At the heart of the Christian mystery is the
divine love or *agape*. There is a twofold movement of that love, a movement of descent and
ascent, or of outgoing and return. The divine
love of God the Father is communicated
to us through Christ and in the Holy Spirit, and
that divine love, present and active in us
by the gift of the Spirit, draws us back
through Christ to the Father, where we rest
as his sons in Christ and share the inner life of
the Godhead. Our grace is an incorporation into
Christ and a share in the life of the Trinity. The
two aspects go together, and if we are to consider
the place of Christ in our Christian life, we must
also consider the place of the Trinity.

At once, however, we meet an obstacle. Many

Catholics hesitate to speak freely about the three persons of the Trinity or assign to each a distinct role in the Christian life, lest they should offend against the unity of the Godhead. This hesitation deprives them of a real awareness of the three as distinct persons, an awareness which should penetrate all Christian piety. Such a timidity about the Trinity is unwarranted. True, the liturgy does not separate the divine persons. It contains no feast in honour of one person by himself. The feasts of Christ are directed to the second person as incarnate, and Pentecost is the celebration of an event, namely, the visible coming of the Holy Spirit. At the same time, the liturgy is filled from end to end with an awareness of the persons as distinct, and it speaks differently of each in relation to the Christian life. We should do the same, confident that, in doing so, we are simply following the purest Christian tradition.

Admittedly, to explain theologically this traditional way of speaking is not easy. It is a truth past doubt that all created effects, whether in nature or of grace, are produced by God as one, that is, by the three persons in so far as they are identical with the one Godhead. The reason for this is clear. The unity of God demands that the persons be distinct only by their mutual relationships. And so, the divine perfections by which they cause created effects are identical in all. How then can we assign the persons distinct roles in our Christian life?

We can do so first by what theologians call

appropriation. To appropriate is to refer to one person what is common to all three in reality. We appropriate, for example, creation to God the Father, though all three persons created as one. This might seem an arbitrary procedure. In fact, it is not. First, we are guided in our use of appropriation by revelation. We appropriate to a person what we find assigned to him continually in the sources of revelation. Secondly, as theologians have observed, the basis of appropriation is a real resemblance between what is appropriated and the personality of the divine person to whom it is appropriated. The use of this procedure, therefore, is a real help to us in envisaging the divine persons and their respective places in the inner life of the Trinity.

Whenever we refer the production of a created effect to one person, it can be only by appropriation. This principle holds good for all the created gifts of grace. But theologians are increasingly dissatisfied with appropriation as a total explanation of the traditional data about the role of the three persons in our Christian life. This dissatisfaction is due in part to a shift of emphasis in the theology of grace. More attention is being given to uncreated grace, which is now seen as the primary constituent of the state of grace.

What distinguishes the order of grace from the order of nature? It is that God gives us, not merely his created gifts, however wonderful these may be, but also himself. Grace is first and foremost the self-gift of God. In a mysterious way, God communicates his own reality to us.

We enter into the possession of God. We are joined to God as he is in himself, and this union with God, by which he is in us as our own, is the primary feature of the state of grace. We call it the indwelling of the Trinity or, less frequently, uncreated grace. Sanctifying grace or created grace is necessary to achieve this union. It is not itself the principal gift in the order of grace. That gift is God himself. But God cannot communicate himself to us unless he brings about in us a real change by which we are made actual recipients of the divine reality. To put it a little differently, when two things are united, one at least must change. If there were no change in either, there would be no real difference between union and separation. God cannot change. Therefore, if we are to be really united to him, we must change. Created grace is the real change in us which ensures the reality of our union with him. It is the bond that binds us to him. However, what comes first is the self-gift of God, which the created grace makes possible.

If we look at the state of grace in this way, we see that we cannot reduce the role which the three divine persons have in our Christian life to the production of the created gifts of grace. In causing these gifts, they act as one. But they give these gifts in order to give themselves. There is a self-giving of God by which he becomes present to us in his intimate reality. The created gifts are such as to establish us in a union with God in which we reach the three persons as distinct. We are joined to each of the three persons by a real personal relationship. Each has a distinct role in our Christian life, not by causing some effect not caused by the other two, but by being present to us as the term of a relationship proper to him. And so, the Father is our Father, and our relationship to him is not the same as that to the other two persons. We are sons in the Son, who is the exemplar of our life as sons of the Father. But we cannot be united to the Father and Son in this way, unless we are joined to the bond of love between them, the Holy Spirit.

The existence of these relations, or perhaps better, this triune relation to the triune God, does no violence to the unity of the Godhead. It accords better with the way the liturgy speaks of the three persons in their relationship with Christians. Appropriation, while necessary, seems inadequate by itself. Needless to say, the matter has been simplified here, and anyone versed in theology will want to ask further questions. The aim has been simply to point to these recent developments in the theology of grace in order to dispel any qualms that might have been felt before a frankly trinitarian account of the Christian life. We may now return to the structure of that life as reflected in the liturgy.

The starting-point is the eternal love by which the Father loved us, his sinful creatures, and willed to save us. The word "love" has been so debased in modern usage that many writers prefer to use the Greek word *agape*, which is the word used in the New Testament for this divine love. The occasional use of the Greek term helps us to remember that the word "love" is intended to have the resonance it has in its biblical context. This gratuitous and utterly selfless love, hidden from all eternity in the depths of God, is common to all three persons of the Godhead, for it is identical with the divine nature with which the persons are one. But we are right to speak of it as the love of God the Father in a special sense. The other two persons have it from the Father, since they proceed from him and have the divine nature from him. The Father remains the ultimate personal source of that boundless love which lies at the origin of our salvation.

The Father willed to impart his love to us through Jesus Christ. Christ came first in the divine plan. The Father willed to send his beloved Son into creation, so as to be the basic principle in creation from which the divine life could be given to men. A person who loves wants to give himself to another and share his life with him. God's eternal plan of love was to give himself to men in such a way that men as a corporate body would be joined to him so closely that they shared the life of the Godhead. To do this he first willed the foundation of the structure into which men would be built and through and in which they would share the divine life. That foundation was the man Jesus, the incarnate Son of God.

The Incarnation is the highest possible communication of God to a creature. God the Son began to exist as man, and the man Jesus was God the Son himself. The created human nature belonged to God the Son and existed in him as his human nature. Here was a union so close that a man was one being with God. A man existed who was no other than the divine person of God the Son. This man is the principle inserted into created reality from which every further communication of divine love comes. He is given as the basis of that structure which is to be formed by men who share the divine life. They have to be built into him. The divine love comes to us through him, and we have the divine life by being made one with him. The Incarnation is the source of our salvation. We were chosen by God in Christ. He called us to be sons in his Son. He sent his Son to be our brother and our head.

God so loved us that he sent his only-begotten Son into this world. The descending movement of divine love is from the Father through the Son whom he sent. But Father and Son are united together in the Spirit, who in the inner life of the Godhead is the bond of love between the Father and the Son. Consequently, the man Jesus, the incarnate Son of God, is united to the Father in the Spirit. The human nature of Christ was filled with the Spirit, who united him as man to his heavenly Father.

We have to be brought to the Father with Christ. It is the function of the Spirit, as the bond of love, to unite us to Christ and join us to the Father through our union with Christ. The Spirit, who is in Christ, comes forth from Christ into us, in order to incorporate us into Christ. Joined to Christ in the Spirit, we go in the Spirit through Christ to the Father. The Father, who sent the Son, sends also the Spirit through the Son, and the Spirit brings us through and in Christ to the Father.

But this movement could not immediately follow the Incarnation. At the Incarnation, God, the Son entered a sinful world and submitted himself to conditions of existence that were the result of sin. Entirely free from sin and himself the incarnate Son of God, the man Jesus should by right have had from the outset a glorified human nature in which the Spirit deployed the full effects of the divine life. But he humbled himself and accepted in obedience to his heavenly Father a solidarity with mankind in the condition in which sin had left it. He was made like us in all except sin itself. He became subject to suffering and death. He wanted to overcome sin, suffering and death by his obedient love. His purpose was to transform his solidarity with us in the flesh into a solidarity of glory in the Spirit. "Flesh" is here used in its Pauline sense to mean man in his weakness and mortality, in his distance from God. Christ took on the likeness of sinful flesh and became one with us in our wretched state. He then transfigured this state in himself and made it possible for us to do the same by being incorporated into him.

And so, although the Spirit was present in Christ from the beginning, the Spirit in him was tied. His full effects were not produced in Christ until the Resurrection, and the Spirit was not given to us until Christ had been glorified. The difficult journey of Christ to the Resurrection, and its release of the Spirit, constitute a movement of redeeming love.

The coming of Christ meant that the eternal love of God was made present in this world, incarnate in the man Jesus. Jesus Christ as God the Son is the perfect expression of the Father, and so the mystery of the self-giving love of God was made known to us in Christ. The love which Christ had for us and by which he gave himself for us is the expression in human form of the divine *agape*. But as imparted to us in Christ, it becomes at the same time a movement of response in man by which man is drawn towards the Father and into the inner life of God. This movement of return, however, had to pass through suffering and death. The divine *agape* in Christ and in men became a suffering love. Having accepted the conditions of our sinful existence, Christ began the painful journey back to his Father. He came into conflict with sin and the forces of evil. These brought him to the Cross. But the free and obedient love with which he accepted his death transformed apparent defeat into victory. It changed his death into a sacrifice, a symbol or expression of that interior surrender by which man enters into union with God in adoring worship. Since the man who made the offering was God, the sacrifice was infinite in value. The human love from which it sprang was not only the most perfect human love, the fullest expression in man of the divine *agape*, but also the act of a divine, not human, person. And so, that sacrifice was of such consummate perfection that it more than made reparation for all the sins of mankind and earned for Christ and for the human race he represented the full fruits of the Spirit. He passed from death to life and broke the barrier between man and God.

By the Resurrection, the outcome of his death, Christ reached the end of his journey back to the Father and entered a new form of existence. The Spirit in him was released. He himself became so penetrated with the Spirit as to be a life-giving Spirit. From his glorified humanity, there streamed forth the Spirit upon men. There could take place now the movement of which we have spoken. The Spirit flows forth from the risen Christ and as a dynamic principle seizes hold of men and incorporates them into Christ so that they share his life. We become with Christ two in one Spirit. As, when a body grows, the new cells are animated with the life of the whole, so, when we are fitted into Christ and become one with his body, we are animated with his Spirit and live with his life.

And the life we receive is the life of sons. Inserted into Christ, we share the divine life by sharing his sonship. We become adopted sons of the Father, embraced by his love for his only-begotten Son, Jesus Christ. The Spirit we receive is the Spirit of adoption who moves us in Christ towards God the Father as our Father. And there we rest in an eternal exchange of love.

But our incorporation into the risen Christ and

our movement towards the Father are not completed in a moment. They are only gradually achieved, and our final assimilation to Christ will not be reached until the resurrection of our bodies. The process by which we become one with Christ and move towards the Father involves our reliving in ourselves the drama of Christ's return to his Father. We must die with Christ and rise with him. We must enter into his sacrificial surrender. We must become one with the suffering Christ if we are to become one with the Christ of glory.

What then are our relations with the Trinity and with Christ? The position of Christ as mediator is central. From all eternity we were called and chosen in Christ. In his love for us, the Father called us to be sons in his Son. We receive our share in the life of God by incorporation into Christ. Our share is a share in his life, and all grace comes to men through his risen humanity. Exalted to the right hand of God by his resurrection, he is the head from which life flows to the body. He is our Lord who, having shown us the way, now rules over us and guides us. He is ever present to us and where there is grace, there is also his active influence. He is our brother and the exemplar of our life.

The gift which comes to us from the Father through Christ is the Holy Spirit. He is the dynamic principle of our life, who unites us to Christ and draws us in Christ to the Father. He is himself the gift *par excellence,* and his indwelling presence brings us all the other gifts and blessings which belong to us as sons of God.

The Father is our Father as the ultimate personal source of our life and the ultimate end towards whom our life tends. As his adopted sons, we are bound to him in a union of friendship and love, joined to him in Christ by the Spirit, the bond of love.

And so, that twofold movement of the divine *agape* into which we are taken up is completed. It comes from the Father through Christ in the Spirit and goes by the Spirit through Christ to the Father. Such is the structure of our Christian life.

3

THE HISTORY OF SALVATION

THE new understanding of the mystery of salvation and the structure of the Christian life depends upon a new awareness that the divine plan of salvation unfolds itself in time as redemptive history. Only when we view redemption as an historical process do we see why the historical events which took place in Christ were necessary for the release of the Spirit. Reflection on the liturgy, again going hand in hand with the progress of biblical theology, has made plain the key place in the Christian scheme of things of the idea known as the history of salvation. But this cannot be grasped without a knowledge of the Old Testament; it was ignorance of the Old Testament that led to its neglect. A renewed sense of the history of salvation has come with the rediscovery of the Old Testament and a greater appreciation of its liturgical use.

The part given to the Old Testament in the liturgy is undeniably large. We have only to look at the commentaries on the Easter Vigil to see that to understand it we need to know the Old Testament. But the use of the Old Testament, though particularly prominent during Lent and Easter, is a feature of the liturgy from end to end.

A knowledge of the Old Testament is necessary, not merely to grasp the liturgical rites of Easter, but also to understand the liturgy of the Eucharist, of baptism and of the other sacraments. Everywhere in the liturgy, we meet the themes and symbols of the Old Testament.

This fact presented the liturgical movement with a serious problem. The approach of the liturgy is far removed in this respect from the outlook of the ordinary Catholic. Among Catholics, the general ignorance of the Old Testament is immense. How then, it was asked, could they be brought to appreciate the liturgy? Should, perhaps, the liturgy be adapted to their present mentality? The temptation was strong to argue that, since people are no longer familiar with the Old Testament, the wiser course would be to present Christian truths to them in a different fashion and modernize the themes and symbols of the liturgy. Such a solution was emphatically rejected. All are at one in laying down as a definite requirement of the liturgical renewal that the people should know the Old Testament and know it as a whole. It is realized well enough that not all can or need have a scholar's understanding of it, but the Old Testament must be familiar once again to our Catholic people in all its distinctive parts. Far from deploring the part given to the Old Testament in the liturgy, writers have expressed regret that in the Roman liturgy we do not have more readings from the Old Testament on occasions when the people are present. Considerable efforts have been expended in Ger-

many and France to make the people acquainted
with the Old Testament. For example, the part
played by the Psalms in liturgical prayer has led
to the initiative of the Gelineau Psalms, which
has succeeded in creating a popular psalmody.

But why must we cling to the Old Testament
in this way?

An immediate answer is that the Old Testament is part of the revelation of Christ, a part
which remains permanently valid for us, although it must be read in the light of Christ.
But this answer does not go deep enough. The
fundamental reason for the permanent relevance
of the Old Testament is that redemption in the
concrete is redemptive history. Essential to the
Christian message is a belief in the history of
salvation. We cannot understand the Easter mystery, the Church, the Eucharist or the sacraments
without a sense of that history. Our faith is not a
list of truths divorced from a relationship to time
and history: it tells us the *story* of God's love, a
story which shows God entering into history and
carrying out there his plan.

Now, we cannot see things in this way if we
ignore the Old Testament. There are two reasons for this. First, we can never grasp a history
by studying only the event which forms its
climax. If we do that, we shall not see it as a history at all. And that is what has happened in fact.
The Christian life has become for many a timeless relationship with God, with a list of truths
to be believed and of obligations to be fulfilled.
But that is an inadequate way of looking at the

Christian message. Second, it is the Old Testament which lays down the pattern of the divine intervention in history, so that the New Testament is largely unintelligible without an acquaintance with the Old. When the first Christians endeavoured to understand and express the meaning of Christ and his work, they turned to the Old Testament and found there the facts and themes that gave them the key to his mystery. We must do the same.

Redemption in the concrete is redemptive history. Perhaps it is advisable to dwell on the meaning of this. God did not save men by isolating them from the universe and from the unfolding sequence of human history. If we suppose that he did so, we are excluding the universe and human history from God's redemptive plan. But that plan, we are told by revelation, embraces the universe and the course of human history. It governs these and directs them towards their final goal. That is the reason why salvation has taken place, and is still taking place, within history.

The conception of a divine plan governing history underlies the Old Testament. The very message of the Old Testament is that God intervenes in history to save. He is the Lord of history. He has a plan that governs history, and history is moving towards an end in which God's plan will be achieved. This was quite an original conception of history, involving a linear idea of time, which differed sharply from the cyclic idea held by the Greeks, who thought of time as an everlasting circular course in which everything keeps recurring. It is less strange to us today because the evolutionary cast of modern thought has made the linear conception of time seem the obvious one.

However, redemptive history is not identical with history as a whole. What constitutes the history of salvation is a particular line of events in each of which faith sees the special intervention of God. According to our faith, this sequence of events is the determining factor that controls human history in its entire course. We believe that what determines the course of history and decides its outcome is not the events studied by historians, the deeds or misdeeds of the great heroes of the past and present, the economic, political and social factors that seem so dominant. No, what in fact decides the ultimate issue is a line of apparently heterogeneous events which are often insignificant by the ordinary criteria of the historian but in which faith sees the hand of God, intervening in human affairs to direct them to his purpose and fulfil his plan. Such events were the call of Abraham, the rescue of the Israelites from Egypt, the covenant of Sinai, the call of the Prophets and, above all, the life, death and resurrection of Jesus Christ. Each of the events that make up the line of redemptive history has the contingent, unrepeatable character of an ordinary historical event; they all actually took place within history. But each event contained within itself the action of God, which gave it a transcendent significance. In varying degrees of efficacy, each event had the effect of changing for ever the relationship between God and man. Every event marked a step forward in the carrying out of God's redemptive plan for the human race. Each time, mankind moved nearer the final accomplishment.

The divine plan of salvation governed this universe from the very beginning; it was the reason why God chose this order in spite of his foreknowledge of human sin. But the series of events by which he actually intervened in a special way to bring about salvation and re-establish man's relationship with him began with the call of Abraham. This event marks the beginning of the history of salvation in the proper sense. The Old Testament recounts the preparatory phase of redemptive history, the phase the purpose of which was to make ready the way for Christ. In the Old Testament, we see the gradual unfolding of God's revelation, which came as a progressive revelation; we are given the story of the first phase in the work of our salvation; and there is made clear to us the pattern of the divine saving activity, necessary for us to know if we are to understand the manner of our salvation in Christ.

When we examine the general movement of the Old Testament towards Christ we find that it involved a process of reduction, a passing from the Many to the One. Taken in its full sweep, the movement proceeded from mankind to Israel, from Israel as a whole to the true Israel or the purified Remnant and from the Remnant to the One, Jesus Christ. The movement of the New Testament era follows an inverse direction; it is the time during which all things are recapitulated in Christ. The movement passes from Christ to the first disciples, from the first disciples to all Christians and from Christians to mankind as a whole. Christ himself stands at the centre of redemptive history. All that went before led up to him as the mediator, the representative of the human race, through whom mankind was to make contact with God. And all flows from him. Salvation comes from God through Christ the mediator to his Church, and through his Church to all men who do not refuse his grace.

The New Testament views Christ in the perspective of the history of salvation. We can summarize its message in this way: Jesus is the centre of redemptive history; he has brought the decisive intervention of God; in him has been fulfilled the expectation of the Old Testament; his death and resurrection are the great central events of all time; salvation has been accomplished; all that went before led up to him, all that comes after depends upon him. The different writers of the New Testament put into relief various aspects of the mystery of Christ, but common to all is this conviction of the place of Christ in the history of God's saving activity.

The definitive intervention of God in history took place in Christ. Nothing else remains to be done but to allow what was accomplished in

Christ to exert its full influence. Consequently, the coming of Christ introduced the last days, and we must say that the final era of history is now here. Everything needed for salvation was given in Christ: the full revelation of God, the complete reparation of sin, the power to regenerate this universe and transform it into a new creation. Nevertheless, the effects of Christ's work are to be deployed only gradually, so as to allow men to co-operate with this work of salvation. The co-operation of men is utterly dependent on Christ but the possibility of it is given by grace as a sign of God's respect for the dignity and freedom of man. This means that an intermediate period, the period of the Church, comes between the historical events of Christ and that final state of glory which will be the full effect of his work. And we live in that period.

We are in the midst of redemptive history. Behind us is the past with the mighty deeds of God for our salvation, culminating in the events of Christ. The present is the age of the invisible rule and influence of the risen Christ. He reigns over men, although his rule is not yet fully manifested. During this period he is gathering his own to himself. Before us is the glory of the future, already in a sense present in Christ, but still awaiting its full disclosure at the Second Coming, when Christ will come again and bring all to its final achievement.

The sense of the history of salvation should pervade our lives as Christians. We must look back to the past, to the events of Christ, for we receive grace in virtue of what was done once for all by Christ. We should live in the present with a consciousness that, joined to the risen Christ, we are taking part in redemptive history. Our Christian lives are a part of that history. Our hope turns us to the future, because as Christians we long for the accomplishment of God's plan and the complete manifestation of Christ's glory, and it is only then that we ourselves shall receive the fullness of our salvation in the resurrection of the body. The history of salvation is our own history. Christian initiation introduces us and our lives into the line of redemptive history, so that we take part in the great drama of redemption and enter into the saving plan which God is unfolding in the midst of time.

The whole liturgy is permeated with this sense of the history of salvation. This is particularly true of the Eucharist. Through the Eucharist, the Christian is joined to great saving events of the *past*. Those who take part in the Eucharist share in the present *reality* of salvation and in that way are inserted ever more deeply into the flow of redemptive history. The Eucharist anticipates the *future,* making men ready for the final end and giving them a pledge of the glory to come.

The Eucharist connects us with the past. "Eucharist" means "thanksgiving". To give thanks to God is to recall with gratitude all he has done. The Jews were always telling of the mighty deeds which God had done on their behalf. We have an even greater reason to look back to the death and resurrection of Christ, from which our salvation flows. The Eucharist is therefore the memorial of Christ. But an empty commemoration is not enough. A presence is demanded. We are saved by being joined to Christ and to the actions by which he saved us. For this we need the presence of Christ and of his saving deeds. This is brought about.

Christ is present in the Eucharist. The risen Christ is there with all the power he possesses as the conqueror of sin and death. But more than this. He brings his sacrifice. The sacrifice of the Cross is given to us as the sacrifice of the Mass. The Eucharist carries the past into the present and so continues the history of salvation. The sacrifice of Christ becomes the sacrifice of the Church. And Christ in the Eucharist gathers around himself the new People of God. This sacred meal makes men the one body of Christ. Since the design that governs history is to unite men in Christ, the Eucharist is the carrying out of that design, and by it redemptive history is sent forwards to its final end.

And at Mass we assemble to wait for the coming of Christ. The Eucharist looks to the future and is a pledge of the future. While we wait for him in hope, Christ is present with us unseen. He celebrates with us here and now the messianic feast. This anticipation we enjoy is a promise of future glory. Through the Eucharist we belong already to the world to come.

And so, the Eucharist joins the past to the present, fills the present with the life of Christ and strengthens those who wait in hope with a glimpse and taste of the future. It exists and acts in the context of the history of salvation.

The same applies in varying degrees to the whole of the liturgy. To try to understand the liturgy without an awareness of the history of salvation is as hopeless a task as to try to appreciate a symphony when tone-deaf. But here the liturgy simply reflects the essential structure of the Christian revelation and the permanent framework of the Christian life. The Christian revelation is not a series of abstract truths but the story of the events by which God intervened in human history, together with a statement of the significance of these events for us. The Christian life is not a timeless relationship with God, but the taking part in an unfolding scheme of redemptive history, the full accomplishment of which will coincide with the fullness of our own individual salvation.

4

THE CHURCH

I N the words of Pope Pius XII in *Mediator Dei*, the liturgy "is the public worship which our Redeemer, the head of the Church, offers to the heavenly Father and which the community of Christ's faithful pays to its Founder, and through him to the eternal Father; briefly, it is the whole public worship of the mystical body of Jesus Christ, head and members". This magnificent definition is an outstanding advance on the rubrical notion of the liturgy, widely current not so very long ago, which made the liturgy the sum-total of the various rubrics and ceremonies belonging to the Mass and sacraments. But if it enshrines a fresh insight into the nature of the liturgy, this insight has evidently been gained only by relating the liturgy to the doctrine of the Church. Our understanding of the liturgy flows from our understanding of the Church. When we approach the liturgy in this way, we see that its source is Jesus Christ as head of the Church. It owes its existence and efficacy to him. He is our high priest, but exercising now his priesthood through and with the Church. All the members of his mystical body share in his priesthood and his worship. Consequently, the liturgy is the public worship offered by the whole Christ, head and members.

Any liturgical renewal that is more than superficial is based on reflection upon the mystery of the Church. We are not surprised, then, to find that the leaders of the liturgical movement have given much attention to the doctrine of the Church. However, the revival in the theology of the Church goes back well beyond the present liturgical movement. Historians trace it back to the Romanticism of the nineteenth century, with its stress on life and vital values, and to the work of Moehler and the Tübingen theologians in that setting. Another factor which helped Catholics to an awareness of the mystery of the Church was the struggle with naturalism. At the same time, theological reflection on the Church has been considerably stimulated by the upsurge of interior life within the Church in recent years. The liturgical movement arose as part of this general renewal in the life of the modern Church. Although it found already at its disposal an active theology of the Church, its coming must be counted an important cause of the unfailing vigour with which thought has been devoted to the mystery of the Church. We are right, then, in saying that the liturgical movement and a renewed ecclesiology go together. So closely are the two connected that it would be relevant to give here in some fullness the doctrine of the Church as expounded in modern theology. That is beyond the scope of the present essay, and it must be enough to indicate some points where the liturgy helps us to grasp the mystery of the Church.

We have been talking about the Church as the Mystical Body for years, and there is no doubt that there is a deeper understanding of the Church than existed previously. All the same, we have largely failed to get the full doctrine across. People realize better the mysterious union that unites them to Christ and to each other, but where we have failed is in conveying the identity of the Mystical Body of Christ with the reality of the parochial community as it exists here and now. Our congregations lack a sense of community. Some would say that our most important task is the creation of such a sense of community, and what does that mean but the creation of a sense of the Mystical Body, not as something up in the air but in its concrete realization in the local community? Mr. Smith may have heard of the Mystical Body, but he does not really think it is as a community that we live in Christ, that the Mass is a communal sacrifice and Communion a communal meal which we do and share only together, and therefore he does not see why he should not follow the Mass on his own and ignore the existence of Mr. Brown. In order to bring what we say about the Mystical Body down from the clouds and apply it to the concrete reality of the Church, we need to see the liturgical assembly as the expression and cause of the Church.

We are the Church when scattered in our daily occupations through factories, offices and homes, but when we come together in the Sunday assembly the Church is given its visible expression as a community. Our assembly for Mass is the symbol, the cause and the realization of our union together in Christ. It is all this because it is a eucharistic assembly, that is, an assembly with the Eucharist as its focal point. But we must not dismiss the assembly itself as irrelevant; it is part of the eucharistic celebration. An important function of the Sunday Mass is to gather and express the community. The Church becomes visible, and, in the setting of the gathered community, the Eucharist is celebrated as the sacramental symbol of our unity and its source and cause.

The Mass has a structure that is designed, as historical studies have abundantly proved, to make it a communal celebration and a real expression of the community. The restoration of an active participation of the faithful in the Mass is not a didactic trick, intended simply to help them follow what is going on, but the renewal of a function of the eucharistic assembly that alone explains its structure, and the atrophy of which has resulted in a deterioration of the Christian life of the people: namely, the function of expressing visibly in a communal celebration the Church as the one Body of Christ and the chosen People of God. As long as our Sunday congregations are as amorphous and passive as cinema audiences and our communicants as indifferent to each other as solitary eaters in a restaurant, the doctrine of the Mystical Body has not been understood.

An obstacle to the liturgical movement with its attempts to change the habits of our Sunday congregations is the prevalence of too low, too incomplete a view of the meaning of the liturgical assembly. The latter phrase itself would be considered by many as a highfalutin' way of describing a crowd of people present at Mass. People are aware of the mystery of what takes place at the altar, but not of the mystery of the assembly itself. This, however, is a mystery, and an awareness of its sacred character might shock us into carrying it out more worthily. The assembly is the mystery of the Church made actual as a sacred reality in a concrete time and place. But to understand this we must go back a little and consider the mystery of the Church in a more general way.

The Church comes from above. That is the key principle in Catholic teaching on the Church. The Church is not the creation of man; it is not a society brought about in a human way by the coming together and self-organization of men interested in Christ and his teaching. The Church owes its origin to an eternal decree of God and a special divine intervention in human history, exercised in Christ. The divine decree which is the cause of the Church (and it is a decision prompted by love), is one and the same decree by which God willed to send Christ and bring about our redemption. The Church is the fullness of Christ, the body of Christ. The choice of the Church by God is the choice of Christ our Saviour considered in its full meaning. If Christ is central in the plan of God, so also is the Church, which is the prolongation of Christ. And, as we were called and chosen by God in Christ, so by the same decree we were called and chosen in the Church.

The first origin of the Church is from God the Father. He it is who sends the Son to be the head of the Church. The sending of the Son includes the mission or sending of the Church, so that the Church arises out of the mission of the Son by the Father. When we call the Church the People of God, we are referring it back to God the Father, who sent the Son. When the Son came, he imparted to the Church a participation in his own mission. We can say, then, that the Church exists in the current of life between the Father and the Son and enters into the relationship between the Son and the Father. Christ is the Lord of the Church and the principle of its life. The life of the Church is a share in the life of Christ. But the incarnate Son exists from the Father; so also, then, does the Church.

The work of establishing the Church was completed, and enduring existence given to it, by the sending of the Spirit. Father and Son send the Spirit, and through this sending the Church is given the indwelling presence of the Holy Spirit. The Spirit is the dynamic principle uniting the Church to Christ, conveying the life of Christ to the Church and drawing the Church back through Christ to the Father from whom it came.

So, the Church comes from the Father through Christ and exists in Christ, sharing his relation to the Father. The Spirit, the soul of the Church, animates the Church and gives it its union with Christ, and by the Spirit the Church returns in a movement of love to the Father through the Son. Hence the Church has the trinitarian structure characteristic of the Christian economy and life. It exists in the inner life of the Trinity. Christians share this life by grace, but they share it as a community, as the Church. And we are speaking of the Church as we know it in its historical reality, not of some imaginary invisible Church. The relationship of the Church to the Spirit ensures that it possesses permanently the inner life of grace. But its relationship to Christ, from whom it receives the Spirit, means that the Church as the body of Christ has a visible structure and organization by which it prolongs the Incarnation.

Such is the wonderful mystery of the Church. Now, the sacred and mysterious reality of the Church as inserted into the historical order and present here in this world is given existence on two levels. It exists on the level of a permanent institution and community, and on the level of an event.

The Church is a permanent institution and community, As an institution, it possesses an enduring visible structure that comes from Christ and ensures the conformity of the Church to the Incarnation, and that visible structure is perennially endowed with the saving power of Christ.

At the same time, the Church is a permanent community in which Christians live together in Christ. They possess their life of grace as members of a corporate body, as parts of an organic whole, even when they are physically separated from each other through the conditions of existence in this world.

But it was the will of God that the mystery of the Church should achieve again and again an even greater presence in history, a fuller actuality, in the manner of an event in which its permanent reality would be more clearly manifested and, at the same time, strengthened and created anew. This event is the liturgical assembly and, in particular, the eucharistic assembly. Here the Church is seen as a visible community and its reality given a deeper intensity.

We come together at Mass in response to a call of God the Father. Our assembly is not a merely human gathering, not even if we assert this with the qualification that we come to receive a supernatural gift. Our assembly is created from above by the summons of God the Father. He has promised to send Christ, his Son, when we gather together to celebrate his *anamnesis,* the memorial of his passion, death and resurrection. And this sending of Christ that marks our assembly is a call or demand of the Father, just as the sending of Christ on earth was a call from God that demanded man's response. It is God the Father, through Christ, who has called us together when we come to

Sunday Mass, and our response is due to the action of his Spirit in our hearts.

When we are assembled together in answer to the call of God, God sends us his Word. We do right in this connection to recall the desert assembly of the Israelites at Sinai to receive the Law. The assembly of the People of God is the privileged place for the proclamation of the Word. The Word comes to us in other circumstances also, but the assembly remains the occasion of its principal manifestation. The Word now comes to us from the Father through Christ. Christ is the very Word of God and it is Christ himself with his message that is now proclaimed. And it is the living Christ himself who speaks to us when the Scriptures are read and the homily preached, even though he now uses the voice of his ministers. The ministers of the Church are his representatives; they speak in his name and with his power. Consequently, there is a sending of the Spirit. When the Word is proclaimed, the Spirit is present, opening our hearts and provoking our response. The Word given in the assembly has a dynamic power, because the Spirit is sent into the midst of the gathered community.

But our union with Christ is not established simply by faith in his message, but by effectual contact with his redemptive acts. The saving activity by which the Church continues the work of Christ does not consist solely in the Word as preached but in the Word as sacramentally efficacious. So, in our assembly, the reading and

preaching of the Word is followed by the eucharistic celebration, in which the mystery of Christ's
redemptive work is sacramentally renewed, so
that we can take part in it.

The Church owes its existence to the mystery
of Christ. It is founded on his death and resurrection. And its enduring existence is secured
by the sacramental renewal of that mystery. The
Eucharist is the event by which the Church is
given existence and permanence in different
times and places as its reality is extended through
time and space. Through the Eucharist Christ
builds up his mystical body. The effect of the
Eucharist is the corporate reality of our union
with Christ and with each other. Certainly, baptism establishes this union in an initial way. But
it does so only because it depends itself upon the
Eucharist, the centre of the sacramental order.
Baptism exists as a first step towards the Eucharist. It unites us to Christ and the Church, but
by relating us to the Eucharist. The Eucharist is,
as it were, already active in us through baptism.
Union with Christ and the Church remains the
proper effect of the Eucharist, which alone gives
it in full. That is why the Eucharist is a communal celebration. Since the effect intended is
our life as a community in Christ, the celebration by which this is achieved is rightly a communal celebration. It is as a community that we
must enter into the mysteries of Christ by
celebrating them sacramentally and receiving as
a fruit of this our corporate existence in Christ.

There is, then, the closest connection between

the Eucharist and the Church. It is an interesting fact that the term "Mystical Body", now used of the Church, was originally used to designate the Eucharist. The reality of the Eucharist, in the old scholastic sense of the effect achieved by it, is, precisely, the Church, the mysterious reality of our communion of life with Christ and with each other. This reality involves the divine missions and our relationship with the Trinity in the way already explained. And this effect is brought about by a sacramental celebration in which the whole community takes part. Each member of the community does so according to his place in the Church. Only the ordained minister has the power to make present again Christ and his mystery. But the assembly is not extraneous to the celebration, as if the people were watching from without. The assembly is part of the eucharistic celebration and the people are there to join in. It is no historical accident that the Mass in its outward structure and symbolism is designed as the action of an assembled community.

We insist vehemently that the Church comes from above and was instituted by Christ, and yet we sometimes act as if the mystery of the Church can be realized in a particular place by human organizing ability, in the same way as a branch of a political party. In fact, the realization in any place of the mystery of the Church is due to the divine missions, and the place of the divine missions is pre-eminently the liturgical assembly. Just as the Christian initiation of the individual person receives its completion in the celebration and reception of the Eucharist, so also the Church receives its full existence in a given place by the event of the eucharistic assembly. And the continuance of the Church is caused by the continual celebration of that assembly. In it the mystery of the Church is given its expression and inserted ever more deeply into a particular historical situation.

The liturgical assembly is the mystery of the Church as realized in the concrete in a given time and place. It is simply the local Church finding its expression and reaching the fullness of its life in an event. We should, then, expect the assembly to reflect the fluctuations in the life of the Church. The tendency to identify the Church with the clergy and see the laity as passive recipients from the Church rather than active sharers in its life and work has been reflected in the liturgical assembly, which has become largely a clerical affair with the laity as passive onlookers. Those are inconsistent who keep preaching about the Mystical Body and the need for the lay apostolate, and at the same time ignore the desire for active participation in the liturgy. They condemn their preaching to ineffectualness. The liturgical assembly is simply the Church in a given place in its fullest manifestation and greatest actuality. It is there that the individual meets the Church in the concrete. If he is passive there, he will be a passive Christian in other respects. In point of fact the structure of the Mass is designed to give each one in the liturgical assembly the place that corresponds to his place in the life of the Church in general. The efforts of the liturgical movement to reanimate that structure should be seen as an endeavour to give people a new sense of the Church. Without such efforts, the renewed ecclesiology will be the painting of an imaginative picture rather than a description of the actual life of Christians as a corporate body.

5

LITURGY AND MYSTERY

ANY account of the doctrinal side of the
liturgical revival must give a place of
honour to what has been called the theology of mysteries, associated with the work of Dom
Odo Casel, monk of Maria Laach. It was precisely
in seeking to give a satisfying doctrinal basis to
the liturgical movement, with all its desires and
efforts, that Dom Odo was led to the intuitions
and reflections which he set forth in his many
writings and which, by any estimation, must
rank among the most significant influences in
present-day theology. He did not regard himself
as a speculative theologian, offering a new theory
for analysis and debate, but as a simple exponent
of the rich data he found in tradition and the
liturgy. The pattern of a life lived in contact
with the liturgy and centred on the paschal
mystery was completed by the circumstances of
his death. After singing the *Lumen Christi*, he
collapsed while preparing to sing the *Exsultet*.
He died on the morning of the Resurrection,
27 March, 1948.

From the beginning, his work was surrounded
with controversy. Some of the opposition was
uncomprehending and negative; some of it sym-
pathetic but questioning. Casel did not always

express himself clearly or happily. We must distinguish between his fundamental insights and his attempts to formulate and defend them. The former have won increasing acknowledgement; the latter were open to criticism. His great merit is to have clung tenaciously to his basic intuitions despite all resistance. For that, he has earned our respect as a pioneer and will be remembered as the one who inaugurated what is perhaps the most fruitful doctrinal movement of our time. What has happened since is that more and more theologians have put themselves under the banner of the theology of mysteries and are engaged in developing and modifying Casel's ideas and in investigating more thoroughly their basis in tradition. That means that the present situation is complicated. It would take a long book to analyze the writings of those who have written on this subject and to explain the standpoint and ideas of the various authors. It seems more useful to leave aside such a work of analysis and comment and to give instead a brief positive account of the subject-matter itself. The following brief synthesis is necessarily personal in that it does not aim at reproducing exactly the thought of any one writer. At the same time, it does not lay claim to any originality of thought.

The theology of mysteries gets its name from the fact that it expounds the whole saving work of God, and, in particular, the liturgy itself with the help of the concept of "mystery". But it has enriched that concept. We have become accus-

tomed to think of a mystery as a mysterious truth
beyond our reason. We place it exclusively in
the realm of doctrine, and, when we refer to
revelation, we almost always have statements of
doctrine in mind. But, besides revelation as a
message addressed to the mind, there is revelation understood as the divine reality communicated to men and actually present as a saving
force within human history. In this present
order, God does not make himself known to men
merely by issuing doctrinal statements. God
reveals himself by giving himself. He enters
human history, acts within it, and remains present so that man may attain salvation by accept-
ing God's self-gift and submitting to his action.
This coming of the divine reality or saving act
into history constitutes the history of salvation.
Revelation understood as the divine reality in
history is basic; revelation as a message is given
with reference to it, and its purpose is to express
the significance of that reality and to lead us to
it. Likewise, the term "mystery" should mean in
the first place the divine reality as communicated
to men, and then, in relation to this, the doctrinal statement that expresses it. That is how
the word is understood in the theology of mysteries; it indicates the reality of God, hidden
yet communicated.

When we go on to consider the levels of meaning contained in the idea of mystery understood
as the divine reality, we are first led into the
hidden depths of God himself. Ultimately, the
mystery is God himself, holy and utterly other,

inaccessible in his inner life to man as man. But the word "mystery", while it expresses the hidden character of God with his eternal love, evokes the fact that God has revealed himself and communicated his love. He did so in Christ. For us, the mystery is the Christian mystery, the mystery of Christ. The action by which God saved us took place in Christ; the communication of the divine reality to men was given in and through Christ; all the saving acts of God in history are ordered to Christ and dependent upon what was realized in him. Christ, in what he was, in what he did, in what was realized in him, is the mystery in the basic sense; he is the divine reality present in history to save.

We can speak in the plural of the mysteries of Christ, because all that Christ was and did is included in the mystery of Christ. We can distinguish the different elements of his mystery and refer to the mystery of the Incarnation, of the Birth, of the Passion, of the Resurrection and so on. At the same time, we must not lose sight of the unity of the mystery. Rich in many elements and aspects, it is a whole; there is but one mystery. But how are we to express it in its unity? It is inadequate to see it simply as the person of Christ. The events of Christ, his saving work, are essential to the mystery and cannot be excluded from it. The mystery is a divine saving action achieved in Christ. Now, when we try to see the events of Christ as a unity, tradition leads us to group them under the idea of a *transitus*. The word simply means a *passing* from one order to another. The divine love or *agape,* which is the saving force of God, came down into this world in Christ. Christ was God the Son incarnate. The man Jesus, as God the Son, was filled with the Spirit of Love, which moved him towards God his Father in a surpassing act of love and obedience. Yet, at the beginning, the man Jesus belonged to this order of sin and death. Himself utterly free from sin, he had submitted himself to the conditions of this world ruptured by sin. He achieved its redemption by a movement of return under the power of the Spirit to his heavenly Father. The return involved a struggle with the forces of evil. In the course of it, the divine love in Christ found expression as a suffering love and culminated in the self-surrender of a sacrificial death. At the climax, in the Passion and Resurrection, Christ broke free from this world dominated by sin and death and passed into the new order of the Resurrection. The *transitus* took place; man in Christ passed from death to life, from this world to the next, from time to eternity, from corruption and suffering to glory. This was the act of God's saving power as realized in Christ. This was how the act of divine love was inserted into history and the dynamic reality of God's life communicated to mankind in Christ. The *transitus* of Christ was continued by his ascension and exaltation to the right hand of God; it will be finally completed in the *parousia* or Second Coming, when the glory of Christ now extended into his body, the Church, will be fully manifested. Such is the mystery of Christ, stretching from the Incarnation to the *parousia,* with the Death and Resurrection as its climacteric.

What was done in Christ must be done also in us. We too have to pass from the order of this world of sin and death to the order of the Resurrection. But the *transitus* in us cannot be a new salvation; it is the one salvation achieved by Christ. We must be taken up into the movement of Christ. We must share in his death and resurrection for only in Christ can we be saved. If so, we must make contact with the mystery of Christ. Although it took place in history, it must in some way be made present to us, so that we can be inserted into it. It is made present to us in the liturgy. The liturgy is, then, a further level of the mystery. It is the mystery of Christ made present to us in the Church so that we can share in it. The mystery of Christ becomes present sacramentally. By a symbolic representation of the saving work which Christ accomplished historically in the past, it makes that saving work really present; it reactualizes it, so that we can join ourselves to it and thus reach salvation. Hence the theology of mysteries, in considering the liturgy, considers it above all as a mystery and means by this that the liturgy is a symbolic re-enactment of the mystery of Christ which brings present the one, unrepeatable reality of that mystery itself. Through the symbolic representation, we enter into the unique mystery.

It is an axiom of this approach that a man

65

does not become a Christian by the mere acceptance of the teaching of Christ, nor by the mere acceptance of graces communicated by Christ, but by a real share in the very saving activity of Christ. We are inclined to think of the saving work of Christ, the mystery of Christ in the full sense, as something in the past in which we have no part. We benefit from it, in the sense that Christ, through what he did, is now able to give us all the graces that we need to get to heaven. But we regard ourselves as recipients of the grace of Christ rather than as reliving the mystery of Christ. Casel and his followers insist that we are Christians only because there is realized in us what was realized in Christ. The mystery of Christ extends also to us and embraces us, so that we not merely receive grace from the saving work of Christ, but also enter into that work itself. Hence we must make contact, not only with Christ and his grace, but also with the saving acts of Christ. We do this in the liturgy, in which the saving acts of Christ are made present sacramentally. This teaching of the theology of mysteries means that it involves an all-embracing conception of the Christian life itself, and is not simply an interpretation of the liturgy.

But that brings us to the problem around which discussions are still taking place. If we are to enter into the saving acts of Christ, they must be made present to us here and now. It is asserted that they are made present in the liturgy. But in what sense? And how can saving acts which were realized as events in the historical order be made present here and now? It seems best to tackle the problem by outlining step by step what can be said.

The saving mystery of Christ is rendered present in the liturgy in the sense that, in the liturgy, what was done in Christ is done in us by the action of Christ. Very often we think of grace in a static way, almost as a sort of fluid poured into the soul as into a vessel when we receive the sacraments. It is indeed a quality inherent in the soul, but it is at the same time a dynamic force that penetrates and changes our being and then impels us onward in a movement of loving return to the Father. Moreover, we must remember that created grace does not stand by itself as the sufficient explanation of our new existence as sons of God. It raises us to the divine life only because it is a unitive reality which serves as a bond or link establishing our union with the Holy Spirit, who is given to us and dwells within us. The Holy Spirit, who comes to us by grace, unites us to Christ, relates us in Christ to the Father as our Father and moves us in Christ towards the Father in a movement that will only reach its completion in our beatitude and glorious resurrection. The reception and increase of grace must not be thought of as the passive reception of an inert gift. What happens is that we are swept up into a movement that transfers us from the order and dynamism of this world into the order of the Resurrection and the dynamism of the Spirit. Consequently, our reception of grace is the taking place in us of that same process which, considered in its full corporate universality, we call the history of salvation, and, considered in Christ, constitutes the mystery of his redemptive work.

All this means that the mystery of Christ is reproduced in us. The *transitus* of Christ takes place in a similar way in ourselves. What has happened in Christ the head now happens in the members of his body. The mystery of Christ is extended to them, is continued in them. And this is achieved in the liturgy. In baptism, we die with Christ and rise again with him. We are conformed to Christ in his redemptive action inasmuch as the counterpart of his death and resurrection is enacted in ourselves. What occurs in baptism is the mystery of the death and resurrection, first realized in Christ and now realized in us. It is the same mystery, though with the difference called for by the difference between ourselves and Christ. Likewise, the Eucharist is the sacrifice of the Church in which the sacrificial offering found in Christ is now realized as the sacrificial offering of the Church. And so on with the rest of the liturgy. The saving acts of Christ are present in the liturgy in so far as they are now accomplished in us.

The mystery of salvation is accomplished in us through the action of the glorified Christ. The Spirit we receive is the Spirit of Christ, and all that is achieved in us is due to the activity of the risen Christ, the source of the Spirit. Christ is present in the liturgy, in the Eucharist by his substance, elsewhere by his action, and, present, he brings about in us by his power the return to the Father which he himself achieved.

But however true all this is, it is not an adequate explanation by itself. It leaves in the background the historical work of Christ. Were there nothing more to be said, this work would only indirectly affect us. The events which took place once for all in Christ would have placed Christ in a position in which he could bring about in us a similar passing to a new existence. Having attained glorification as head of mankind, Christ would now be possessed of all power to achieve in us our resurrection to a new life. But the unique events of his life, death and resurrection would not themselves directly influence us. Nor would they in themselves be present in the liturgy, but only in their reproduction in us. The inadequacy of this is particularly felt in regard to the Eucharist, which is not simply the sacrifice of the Church, realizing anew the offering of Christ, but the very sacrifice of Christ rendered present before us.

Can we speak then of the presence in the liturgy of the very historical work of Christ? Is there any sense in which we can say that the events which occurred once for all in Christ are made present in the liturgy in their unique, unrepeatable reality? We can turn for help here to a point taught by St. Thomas, which has been brought into prominence once more in theology. St. Thomas said that the events of Christ were causes of what takes place in ourselves when we receive the gifts of salvation. Our resurrection, for example, is brought about by the resurrection of Christ. He did not mean only that our resurrection is due to the action of the risen Christ now reigning in glory, but that our resurrection is effected by the causal influence exerted by the event itself of Christ's resurrection. The saving acts realized in the past in Christ and forming his historical work are permanently influential. All that occurs in us is due to their efficacy and power. We have seen that the mystery of grace reproduces in us what took place in Christ. Now we must add that it takes place under the causal influence of what took place in Christ. The mysteries that constitute the historical work of redemption exert on us here and now in the liturgy a power through which the work of redemption is accomplished in us.

But how can what belongs to a given time and place be actually operative in men far removed from that time and place? The answer lies in the fact that the principal cause is always God. What is true of the glorified Christ as cause of grace is true also of his historical work as cause: in both instances, the causality is a subordinate causality. The action of the historical work of Christ, when it bestows grace upon us, is subordinate to the action of God. It is subordinate in the way the action of an instrument is subordinate to the action of its user. Since God is immediately present and his action is the principal factor involved, he can establish the causal relation required between the work of Christ and ourselves. He can act on us through the historical work of Christ and make the process of salvation in us dependent on the events of Christ. Through the divine action we are brought into contact with the saving work of Christ and placed under its influence.

In the liturgy, therefore, we make contact with the saving acts of Christ. In that sense they are present in the liturgy. We can speak of a virtual presence, which means a presence of power, a dynamic presence. The risen Christ is present in the liturgy because he acts upon us. It is through him that God gives us grace, and it is through him that God establishes contact between us and his historical work. But in the liturgy, not only the risen Christ, but also the historical work of Christ, the saving events enacted in Christ, act upon us. Consequently, there is also a presence of this work, of these events. For example, the death and resurrection of Christ are made present in the sense that they exert upon us an actual causal influence. And we can say that the total mystery of Christ, the entire saving work of Christ, is present in the liturgy by such a virtual or dynamic presence.

Already this is much and in vivid contrast to the impoverished view of the liturgy so often proposed. Even so, reflection carries us further. The historical work of Christ cannot be present as historical except by a virtual presence. What took place in the past as an historical event can only be present here and now in the way that has just been explained. But while the mystery of salvation was realized historically in the unique events of Christ's life, death and resurrection, its reality on its deepest level transcended history. What was its deepest reality? It was the enduring act of love in Christ. The mystery of salvation is the mystery of the divine *agape*. This came into the world in Christ and found expression in the human love of the incarnate Son of God. Governing all the life of Christ was a sublime act of charity, found in Christ's human will from the beginning of his human existence and enduring unchanged until now. It was this act that lay behind all that Christ did and penetrated it with its influence. It gave redemptive value to all the events of the *transitus*; it was their deepest reality. The implications of this act of love unfolded themselves throughout the historical course of Christ's life and commanded his many-sided activity, while ensuring its basic unity. It thus became woven into the web of history; but in itself it transcended history. From the beginning of his human life, Christ enjoyed the Beatific Vision, which exists outside time, and the duration of which is a participated eternity. The act of charity, at its deepest level, was the counterpart in the will of the vision in the intellect, and it has the same timeless and unchanging duration.

This act of love still exists in the risen Christ in heaven in its unchanged reality. The events of the history of Christ formed the expression of it which God had decreed in his eternal plan. Consequently, it remains forever related to those

events; hence the historical work of Christ retains
its unique importance. At the same time, since
it still endures in its supra-temporal reality, it
can be made present in the liturgy, where it
finds a sacramental or symbolic expression.
Thus, this act was the act of offering which con-
stituted the sacrifice of Christ on the Cross. When
it is made present in the Eucharist, it ensures
the identity between the sacrifice of the Mass and
the sacrifice of the Cross. The Mass is the sacramental expression of the same offering that was
expressed in the historical order on Calvary.
Elsewhere in the liturgy it is present in a lesser
degree. But, since Christ becomes present to us
throughout the liturgy by his action, the act of
love which is the mainspring of all that Christ
does and which is the mystery of the saving work
of Christ in its timeless and transcendent core is
also made present to us throughout the liturgy.

The liturgy is the mystery of Christ made
present to us. It is a symbolic representation of
the saving work of Christ in which the reality of
that work becomes present. How is it present?
It is present in so far as it is reproduced in us by
the present action of the risen Christ. Our sacramental life is an image of the life of Christ, and
we are conformed to Christ in the mystery of his
transitus. But this is also brought about, not only
by the present action of Christ, but also by the
active influence of the acts that made up his
redemptive work. These are present by their
dynamic power, so that the total mystery of Christ
in its historical realization acts on us in the

liturgy and is the cause of our own participation in the mystery. Finally, the inner core of that redemptive work, since it transcends time, still exists, and hence is made present as an existing reality by means of the liturgical representation.

This presence of the mystery of Christ is found in the liturgy as a whole. And so, the entire liturgy can be brought under the concept of mystery. Nevertheless, the presence is realized in a different way in the different parts of the liturgy. We must understand the presence analogously when we apply it in turn to the Eucharist, the other sacraments, the sacramentals and the liturgical year. The Eucharist holds a pre-eminent place, and there the presence is found in a full sense not realized elsewhere. The other sacraments also occupy a place apart. But all the liturgy is a symbolic representation of the mystery of Christ that to some extent makes present its reality. The principle limiting the degree of presence is the sign itself. The mystery is made present in a way that follows and is in accordance with its symbolic representation.

This account of the theology of mysteries has been extremely brief. Perhaps, however, enough has been said to convey a sense of its richness. Many lines of thought need to be pursued further and much remains to be clarified. But even a brief exposition reveals the intense interest and value of the ideas it has already sent into circulation.

6

SACRIFICE AND SACRAMENTS

IT would be wrong to attribute all the advance that has been made in our understanding of the Eucharist and the sacraments to the theology of mysteries. The development has been extensive and many-sided, and many factors outside the theology of mysteries have contributed to it. It would not even be right to see all the development as an immediate product of the pastoral liturgical movement. Who can analyze the precise causes and interaction of influences that lie behind such developments? The theology of the Eucharist would have been pretty vigorous in any event. However, the important point is the renewal, not its precise causes.

In general, there has been a stress on the dynamic as opposed to the static aspect of the Eucharist. The reason for the Eucharist lies, not in the adoration of the Real Presence, but in its function as sacrifice and food. Since Christ is present in a permanent way, the Church adores him in the consecrated elements. His abiding presence keeps him among us in the tabernacle or monstrance in a special and bodily way that calls forth our devotion and stimulates us to intimate converse with him. Nevertheless, he becomes present in an action that renews sacramentally his act of sacrifice and remains there primarily to nourish us in Holy Communion, so that Mass and Communion are at the centre of any sound eucharistic piety. In other words, the Real Presence was not given as a static presence that finds in itself its own meaning and completion. It has a dynamic purpose: to bring Christ to us in the act of sacrifice and to give him to us as the food of our Christian life. Leave this aside and the Eucharist is deprived of its full reality and chief purpose.

The two aspects, sacrifice and communion, have been brought together and the unity of the Eucharist stressed by the sacramental approach. What this approach means is that the Eucharist is to be understood as belonging in its entirety to the sacramental order; it is sacramental even as a sacrifice. Besides showing the unity of the Eucharist, this new approach has enabled theologians to overcome the limitations of the post-Tridentine theology of the Mass, since it helps to explain how the Mass is a sacrifice without adding to Calvary while yet remaining one sacrifice with it. The nature of the Mass as a sacrifice is to be the sacrament of Christ's sacrifice. It is a sacramental or symbolic representation of the one sacrifice of Christ, but a symbol which brings the reality of Christ's sacrifice really present. Vonier was a pioneer here, but the discussions today are mostly centred on the theology of mysteries, since that theology and the sacramental explanation of the Mass largely coincide.

Much attention has been given to the relation

between Holy Communion and the celebration of the sacrifice. Efforts have been made to restore the idea that, where there is no obstacle, those present at Mass should go to Holy Communion and thus complete their participation in the eucharistic celebration. It should be abnormal, or rather, unusual, since it is always by its nature abnormal, for a good Catholic to attend Mass regularly but only go less regularly to Communion. Now, what has helped to bring this point home has been the realization that in its outward structure, its sacramental sign, the Eucharist is a sacred meal. It was instituted as a meal, and, despite all ritual developments, this basic structure, which embraces all the aspects of the Eucharist, remains the same.

This does not imply any neglect or minimizing of the sacrificial character of the Mass. The Eucharist is a sacrifice. That is an essential part of its meaning, and the Church has simply exercised its lawful pastoral mission in displaying more fully this particular aspect by ritual development. But it remains true, and it is instructive to observe the fact, that the basic framework which carries all the meaning is a sacred meal.

Christ chose for his sacraments certain fundamental human actions. These had a firmness of texture that enabled them to bear an added weight of meaning. He made the common action of bathing into the sacrament of baptism. And in the Eucharist, he chose a meal as the basic human structure which carries all the rest. Since the Eucharist repeats the Last Supper, it is undeniably a meal; and the way the Eucharist was celebrated in the primitive Church made it very plain that this new Christian rite was a sacred meal. Even today, when the liturgy has developed and the hieratic element has become very prominent, for those who look at it with a discerning eye the basic shape of this sacrament is still that of a meal.

Unfortunately, in this age of profane family life and canteen feeding, we have lost the sense of a meal as a human event of social and, indeed, religious significance. It would be wrong to conceive the Eucharist as a meal according to our impoverished idea of what a meal is. A meal is not just the act of eating; it is a communal celebration. It includes, besides eating, actions that express its social character and, for those who live religiously, actions that express dependence on God and thanksgiving for his benefits. The family meal, for example, is, or should be, the centre of family life; and the meal is the natural means of expressing and strengthening other social relationships.

When we turn to the Bible, we find that this action, already deep with human meaning, is made the symbol of the blessings of salvation. Used regularly in the liturgy of the Temple to indicate union with God and enjoyment of divine favours, the meal became, further, the image of that future salvation and happiness to which the Old Testament looks forward. It was the symbol of the joy of the messianic age. When the intimacy between God and his chosen people was stressed, the meal was thought of as a wedding feast. And the climax of the great feast of the Pasch was a family meal as a religious event. This was chiefly a commemoration of the deliverance from Egypt, but it was also seen as the figurative anticipation of the new and definitive redemption awaited in hope.

Christ expressed his message in the context of these ideas. He described his messianic kingdom and the gifts of salvation as a banquet or wedding feast. He made his own symbolism of the Pasch. What is more, his very actions must be seen as full with such a meaning. The meals which Christ ate with his disciples and with others were intended to express the community of life he willed to share with men—and that meant with sinners, so he ate with sinners. These meals with Christ realized already in part that messianic banquet to which men had looked forward in figure and which will be realized in full in the world to come. And that meaning was present with particular force in the meals which Christ took with his disciples after his resurrection.

This is the background against which we must see the Last Supper. We gain a new insight into its significance when we are aware that in it the various themes connected with the biblical symbolism of a meal came together. But to understand more clearly what Christ did at the Last Supper, we must recall the actions which took place at all Jewish meals, particularly if they were of special religious significance. Whatever other rites were added on occasion, two actions were always found. At the beginning of the meal, the head of the table took bread, broke it with a short blessing and gave a piece to all at table; in that way all present were drawn together for the communal celebration. Then, at the end of the meal, came the blessing, or principal table prayer. Since for the Jews a blessing was thanksgiving, this blessing was a long prayer of thanks, a "eucharist", recounting in biblical fashion the mighty deeds which God had done for his people. On solemn occasions, it was associated with a special cup of wine, the cup of blessing, which the head of the table held high in his right hand during the thanksgiving and then passed round to all present in order to seal their common participation in the feast.

Now, Christ must often have done these two actions at table with his disciples. He would have given a new content to his "eucharist" by including in it his message of salvation. He did them once more at the Last Supper, most probably as part of the more solemn ritual of a paschal meal. But this time there was a striking alteration. He declared the bread to be his body and the wine to be his blood, and gave them as such to his disciples.

But the full significance of this last, farewell meal came from the fact that it celebrated the death of Christ. His approaching death dominated the occasion. The bread represented his body as given for us; the wine, his blood as poured out for us. In giving his disciples his body and blood as food and drink, Christ gave

them what he first offered to his heavenly Father
as a redeeming victim for them. He expressed his
sacrificial offering in symbolic action. He thus
made the sacred meal the sacrament of his sacrifice. Hence, the Eucharist is a sacred meal which
celebrates sacramentally the sacrifice of Christ
and nourishes men on its eternal life-giving
victim.

But if Christ gave us his sacrifice in that way, it
was so that we should join ourselves to it and make
it our sacrifice as well. The study of the liturgy
has led to a better understanding of the Mass as
the sacrifice of the Church. This is the truth
rightly stressed by Fr. Jungmann when he deals
with the meaning of the Eucharist in his great
work *Missarum Sollemnia*. Surprising though it
may seem, what appears most prominently in the
eucharistic liturgy is not that the Mass is the
sacrifice of Christ but that it is our sacrifice, the
sacrifice of the Church, the offering in which we
all share.

In the Mass, it is as head of the Mystical Body
that Christ exercises his priestly office. Hence
the sacrifice is offered by the whole Church; not
by Christ alone as on Calvary, but by Christ with
the Church acting in union with him. The
Eucharist is the sacrifice of the Church, not
simply because the Church possesses it, but because the whole Church offers it. Christ acts, indeed, through specially appointed ministers, but
in a true sense the sacrifice is the sacrifice of all
the faithful. All the members of the Church, the
Mystical Body, enjoy a certain priesthood, a share

in Christ's priesthood, by which they are enabled to share in the sacrifice of Christ.

It is understandable that the liturgical movement has served to focus attention on the question of the share in the priesthood of Christ common to all the members of the Church and on the part played by the faithful in the sacrifice of the Mass. But how do the laity share in the priesthood of Christ? And what is their precise part in the offering of the Mass?

We shall never understand the Christian priesthood, unless we realize, and vividly realize, that in the New Covenant there is but one priesthood, the priesthood of Jesus Christ. He is the one priest of the New Law, and to study the Christian priesthood is to study this one priesthood of Jesus Christ in the full range of its existence and activity.

Christ is our priest. He came as a priest, fulfilling all the figures that went before, and his redemptive mission centred in the redemptive sacrifice of Calvary. It was as a man that Christ was priest, but his priesthood has its source and basis in the Hypostatic Union. The real consecration, the sacerdotal anointing of Christ, is given to his human nature by the grace of union whereby that nature is hypostatically united to God the Son. And the graces necessary for Christ to fulfil his role as priestly mediator between God and men spring from that union.

The priesthood of Christ, however, is not exhausted by his own personal existence and activity. Christ lives in the Church. The Church is the body of Christ, the prolongation and continuation of Christ—and, consequently, of Christ the priest. The Church is the priestly Body of Christ; it is a sacerdotal organism because it is the extension of Christ the priest.

In what way does the Church continue the priesthood of Christ? Since the Church is the body of Christ, all the members share in the priesthood of the head. The Church is the sacerdotal organism, a royal priesthood, and priesthood is co-extensive with it as the priestly body of Christ. But it is shared differently by different members, because the Church is a hierarchical body. The entire Church shares in the priesthood of Christ, organically or according to a unity, but, at the same time, analogically or according to different imperfect participations of the one perfect priesthood of Christ.

There are two ways of sharing in the priesthood of Christ, by baptism and by holy order. The priesthood of Christ comes first: what we find are two different ways of participating in it. To understand the difference and the relation between these two, we must distinguish two aspects of the Church.

The first aspect we encounter in the Church is the official representation of Christ. This is the Church in its hierarchy, in its official mission of making available the visible sources of grace, whether by transmitting with authority the words and orders of Christ or by administering the sacraments; in brief, the Church as representing visibly and authoritatively the Christ who remains hidden until the Second Coming. The second aspect of the Church is communion with Christ. This is the Church receiving all from Christ and entering into his life. It is the Church as the community built by grace, with the task of becoming one with Christ in a union of life and love.

To the first aspect of the Church corresponds the ministerial and hierarchical priesthood given by the sacrament of holy order. This makes men priests as instruments of Christ, endowed with power to perform the visible acts of sacrifice and sacrament. To the second aspect of the Church corresponds the general priesthood of the faithful given by baptism. This confers a capacity for union with the sacrifice of Christ and a receptivity for all the graces available in the Church of Christ. It would be wrong to understand the receptivity as a merely passive receptivity; it involves an active acceptance and co-operation whereby the faithful enter into the mystery of Christ and make it their own. We should also notice that the members of the hierarchical priesthood have and exercise this general priesthood in so far as they too are in personal communion with Christ.

The function of priesthood, whether ministerial or general, is not confined to the Eucharist, though the Eucharist is the centre of reference for all its activities. But what has been said is particularly helpful in understanding the respective roles of priest and faithful in the Mass. The essence of the Mass lies in the twofold consecration. This is an act of power and authority by which Christ is rendered present and the visible act of sacrifice accomplished. Considered in this way, it is carried out by the ordained priest alone. The laity do not share in the power of carrying out this act, nor does the priest possess this power as a deputy or representative of the people: the power comes to him by the character of holy order, and in its exercise he is acting in the name of Christ and as his instrument. But that same visible act renders present the offering of Christ in which all are intended to share and which all must make their own. Under this aspect, the laity offer through and with the priest. They offer *through* the priest, who here represents not only Christ but also the members of the Church. They offer *with* the priest because their sentiments of praise, entreaty, expiation and thanksgiving are joined to those of the priest and presented to God by the external liturgical rite. Christ is the chief offerer, but the priest offers and the faithful offer; and it is the offering of the whole Church, head and members, which is signified by the outward sign and displayed in the course of the liturgy.

In brief, the Mass is the offering of the whole Church, and each member has a part in the offering. But the laity can offer only through and with the priest, because the priest alone has the power to perform the consecration, which is the essential act of sacrifice. The role of the faithful is not to represent Christ in his power and authority, but to enter spiritually into communion with his sacrifice.

We must turn now from the Eucharist to the other sacraments. What has been said about the Eucharist as a sacred meal and as the sacrifice of the Church makes it plain that the Eucharist, while being a representation of the mystery of Christ, is also an expression of the life of the Church. The same is true of the other sacraments, and greater prominence has been given to this point in recent theology. If theologians are seeking to understand the connection of the sacraments with the mystery of Christ, they are also being led by the liturgical movement to grasp more fully the human dimensions of the sacraments as signs of the faith and worship of the Church. The exclusive dominance of the notion of cause in the theology of the sacraments has had an impoverishing influence. We do right to insist on the divine power that is operative in the sacraments, but their human side must not be forgotten. Sacramental activity is a human activity, and the sacraments are actions whereby the Church expresses its worship and its faith. They are designed to have a meaning on the human plane of spiritual and social communication. The liturgy is the symbolic activity of a worshipping community, and as such it has deep roots in human psychology and the laws of social life. This connection with the corporate faith and life of the Church means that normally the sacraments should be celebrated as communal events. This enables them to exercise to the full their role of expressing and building up the life of the community.

The function of the sacraments as signs of faith and worship applies also on the level of individual religious experience. The sacraments include a human response to the divine gifts. While it is true to see the sacraments as gifts from God and causes of grace, it is also true that they imply in their very structure a human response to the divine gifts received. The sacraments are, in fact, meeting-places between the action of God and the response of man. We can describe them as encounters, personal encounters, between man and God. And in the sacramental celebration the human response is expressed as well as the divine action and the divine gift. When we receive the sacraments, or better, celebrate the sacraments, we express our faith and our worship, our response and our co-operation.

The world of sacred signs is still largely unfamiliar to our Catholic people. For them the sacraments are simply means of grace. They think of the sacraments as things apart from themselves which pour grace into them provided they place no obstacle. But we cannot separate the sacraments from our own activity. Sacramental activity is human activity in which we express our faith and worship and celebrate both the mystery of Christ and our own part in it. We must see the sacraments as religious symbolic activity in relation to which we are active, not passive. But this means that we must regain an understanding of symbolism and symbolic activity.

To appreciate the sacred signs of the liturgy, Catholics will need a much greater familiarity with the Bible than they have, because the symbolism used in the liturgy is biblical. But the Bible and the liturgy develop the great basic symbols that have always been used by man and correspond to deep human needs. Symbolical thinking is necessary to man. Man cannot subsist and retain mental health on a diet of purely rational and conceptual thinking; the mind must use as well symbols and images. This is particularly true of man's religious life and the requirements of his worship. Religion remains without firm roots in man until the images it uses have exercised their integrating role on the human personality. We are combating the failure of religion in so many today when we initiate people into the symbols of the liturgy, symbols that are human, biblical and traditional. We have presented the faith too exclusively in cut-and-dried formularies and by the use of conceptual analysis and discursive reasoning. The inadequacy here is not merely doctrinal but psychological. There is a lack on the basic human level. It is this lack that is being supplied by a realization of the full human dimensions of the Church's sacramental activity.

But when we think of the sacramental organization (or economy, as it is called), we must not limit it to the seven rites that are in the strict and proper sense sacraments, any more than we must restrict the seven sacraments to what is necessary for validity. No; each of the seven sacraments is surrounded by a great number of rites, lesser signs or sacramentals, and these have their importance. They are not simply decorative accessories. They form the symbolic context of the sacraments and are necessary to display and express the full meaning of the rite. The seven sacraments are not isolated entities; they form a sacramental world. They form a whole with the rites that surround them and depend upon them and draw from their riches. They form, too, a unity with the rites or sacramentals by which the Church develops and expands its divine worship, such as the dedication of churches, funeral rites, blessings and consecrations, and so on; and, naturally, with the Divine Office, which is the extension of the Mass as a sacrifice of praise.

Through this sacramental economy or world of sacred signs, Christ continues the work of redemption and brings his life, death and resurrection to the men in the Church. The connection between sacramental activity, considered as the symbolic activity of a worshipping community, and that same activity considered as the celebration of the mystery of Christ, is established by the sacramental characters. It is because all the members of the Church share in the priesthood of Christ by the sacramental characters that the Church's worship is not simply an expression of its own life but a mystery—a symbolic representation of the mystery of Christ that brings the reality of that mystery present again here and now. The liturgical movement, with its stress on the liturgy as mystery and yet also on the human character of the liturgy, will undoubtedly lead in the future to a much deeper understanding of the meaning and role of the sacramental characters.

Much could be added here on the contribution of the liturgical movement to our appreciation of the individual sacraments other than the Eucharist. But this is more widely known, and it has seemed better to dwell on the basic ideas that should govern all our thinking about the sacraments.

7

ESCHATOLOGY

ESCHATOLOGY means doctrine on the last
things. So often in the past, these have been
understood in a purely individualistic way.
But this is wholly inadequate. Christian eschatology must be placed in the perspective of the
history of salvation. Human history is moving
towards a final end in which the saving plan of
God will reach its full accomplishment. Eschatology is teaching on this final end. Now, a study of
the liturgy has led to the insight that our Christian life should include an eschatological tension.
We should live in the expectation of the coming
of Christ and all that this will bring.

Surprising though it may seem, we should
want the end of the world and look forward to it.
It is an object of our hope. The early Christians
longed for it and were impatient at its delay. But
for them, unlike ourselves, the end of the world
was not a final catastrophe, whether a natural
disaster or one due to the folly of men, but the
triumph of Christ. This will come about by a
free intervention of God.

The death and resurrection of Christ already
mark the beginning of the end of the world. By
those saving acts Christ introduced the final order
of things into this world and into human history.

The new creation has begun. We already have eternal life. We enjoy already the life of the world to come. We live in the last days. No wonder the first Christians were impatient for everything to be settled quickly. But the ascension of Christ and the promise of his return made it clear that, contrary to what many had thought, the end of the world would come about in two stages.

The present age is the first stage. The final order of things now exists, fully in Christ himself, but only in a hidden, incomplete way in the rest of creation. This is an intermediate period. The reason for such a period is to give men the opportunity of associating themselves freely with the new creation and of co-operating with its gradual penetration into the world. When all is ready, at a time known only to God, Christ will come again. His return will mark the second and ultimate stage.

The second coming of Christ will bring into the open the new order that now lies hidden. It will show the meaning of human history and how God has been present in it, directing it to his purpose. Christ will bring all to completion. His return is the end of the world. It is the end, not in the sense of the destruction of all, but in the sense of the final fulfilment of all. By it will be achieved all that God set out to do when he created this universe and man, all that he planned when he sent Christ to save man, and the universe with man. All that is good and valuable in creation and human history will be taken up into the final order. Nothing except sin will be excluded. Such will be the triumph of Christ. It is the reason why God created this world and the end towards which he is directing all things.

We can see now why Christians must hope for the Second Coming. If we believe in Christ, can we do anything else but hope for the day when his work will be completed? Our failure to long for the coming of Christ is a great loss to our Christian life. It means a failure to grasp the cosmic extent of Christ's work. We think of our religion simply as an affair of our individual happiness. That happiness is part of God's plan, but his plan embraces much more than that. Our destiny is but part of a magnificent plan that includes in its wonderful sweep the whole of creation and the whole of human history. The work of Christ will not be complete until all creation has been brought into subjection and until human history, guided by the action of God, has reached its full unfolding. The second coming of Christ marks this triumphant climax.

When Christ comes again we shall all rise from the dead. These bodies we now have will be given back to us, this time for a life without end. There will happen to us what happened to Christ. The resurrection of Christ is the cause and model of our resurrection, and our new, risen life will be a sharing in the risen life of Christ. But there is more to it than that. To understand the importance of the final resurrection, we must see the close connection between it and our present Christian life.

In a way we already share in the risen life of Christ. We do not often think in this way, but what has already been said should have made it clear that in fact our Christian life, our life of grace, is an incomplete share in the life of the glorified Christ. Baptism is a resurrection. If we want to understand it, we have to compare it with the resurrection of Christ and see our baptism as a taking place in us of what happened when Christ rose from the dead. Our Christian life is a life on a new level of existence, and, when we ask what that new level is, the answer is that it is the level of the risen life of Christ, which we shall enjoy in full at the end of the world.

This new life, which we have here and now, is given not only to our souls but also to our bodies. We have developed the habit of speaking of saving our souls or of the life of the soul, so that it is necessary to insist that Christ came not to save souls but to save men. Man is not a soul that, by misfortune, has become stuck to a body but a living unity of body and soul. Even in talking of the Christian life we cannot leave out the body. When we live our Christian life, we live it in body and in soul. But even this is not quite true, because our bodies and our souls do not exist and act side by side but have one life together. When we act as men, we act as body-souls, the two making one whole or unity, and that is the way we live our Christian life. The sacraments affect us as men and their effects penetrate our bodies as well as our souls. Christ told us that it was because we were nourished on his flesh and blood in Holy Communion that our bodies would rise from the dead.

We can see now why the salvation brought by Christ would be incomplete without the Resurrection. The blessed in heaven are not fully men but disembodied souls. They have received the vision of God and have thus received their eternal happiness. They are already the blessed. But their happiness is incomplete until the Resurrection, because only after the Resurrection will they enjoy their eternal happiness, not merely as souls but also as men.

How, then, has Christ given us salvation? He has not given it to us so that we escape death, but so that we overcome death. As Christians we already share the resurrection of Christ, but that does not mean that we shall not die; it means that we shall conquer death by rising again from the dead. There is planted in us the seed of Resurrection. Our bodies have part in our Christian life and in the effect of the sacraments. The result of this is that, although we die and our bodies corrupt, death cannot gain the victory; the seed has been planted, and when the time comes our bodies will rise from the tomb. Then our share in Christ's resurrection will be complete, and death will be no more. It is significant that the fullness of our individual salvation is given to all of us together as a community and at the moment which marks the final achievement of God's plan for the universe.

The hope of the Second Coming should be

present in every Christian life. The presence of this hope causes us to see the world and human activities in a proper perspective and ensures a balanced conception of our own destiny, which includes the resurrection of the body. Now, most would admit that the hope of the Second Coming has not had much place in the lives of Catholics for many years. It is being given a new vigour by the liturgical movement. The reasons for this are not difficult to see in view of what has been said. The renewed sense of the history of salvation is directing our minds to the final end of that history. In the liturgy we enter into the history of salvation and we do so at a stage that is already that of the last days. Hence, a tension to the future is inevitably created. Again, the stress given to the resurrection of Christ draws attention to our own resurrection and to the fact that by it we receive the fullness of our salvation. Further, the greater sense of the corporate character of the Christian life makes us more aware of the corporate elements in eschatology, namely, the Second Coming, the Resurrection, the Last Judgement and the restoration of the material universe.

And, finally, the liturgy gives expression to this hope again and again. The sacraments are signs, not only of the past and the present, but also of the future. They have an eschatological meaning. They point to the final fulfilment of salvation, and the grace they give here and now is a pledge and a foretaste of the glory to come. This is particularly true of the Eucharist. We gather together in the eucharistic assembly to await the coming of Christ. We anticipate that coming and the messianic banquet by celebrating the sacred meal of the Eucharist. And the eating of Christ's body is the pledge and the preparation of the Resurrection.

Not the least, then, of the benefits of the liturgical revival has been to reveal the eschatological dimensions of the Christian life and sacraments.

8

CONCLUSION

A NEW understanding of Christ, and, in particular, of the significance of his resurrection and the role of the glorified humanity; a sense of the history of salvation; an insight into the mystery of the Church as expressed and realized in the liturgical assembly; a fresh approach to the mystery of Christ's saving work and its permanent presence and efficacy in the liturgy; a richer theology of the Eucharist and the sacraments; a reawakening of a fuller eschatological hope: these are some of the doctrinal insights on which the liturgical movement rests. The list does not claim to be exhaustive, but enough is given, it is hoped, to show that we are dealing with a very extensive doctrinal revival, which is influencing most parts of our Christian faith.

There are those who view the liturgical movement, whether with favour or disfavour, as simply an agitation for ritual changes. We are, indeed, living in an age of liturgical reform, and the reasons have been given for this. It is only human to want to see the changes and to see them quickly. Certainly, if anyone denies the need for the reform of the liturgy, he may be in invincible ignorance, but he is definitely out of touch with the mind of the Church. The movement for liturgical reform has been taken over by the authorities of the Church, and taken over in no uncertain fashion. We have had already some remarkable results of this: evening Mass, relaxation of the eucharistic fast, restoration of the Holy Week celebrations, especially the Easter Vigil, numerous vernacular rituals, some with extensive changes in the rites. More is under way, as is openly made known. Indeed, one would have to be pretty ignorant of liturgical history not to see the desirability of changes. But impatience for these changes is obscuring the immense task we face before all these changes, past and future, are properly assimilated. Ritual changes without a corresponding change in mentality will bear little fruit.

We need, then, to set to work to spread abroad the doctrinal insights that motivate the desire for liturgical reform in those who are leading the movement. Serious reflection is required on our part to make our own the doctrinal progress that underlies the liturgical movement, a progress which is bringing about a welcome reorientation in Catholic piety. These ideas must pervade preaching and teaching. People must become familiar with the Scriptures, particularly with the Old Testament, of which many are so sadly ignorant. Above all, what is needed is a new sense of community, not a sense of belonging to the Church as a vast institution—that is common enough—but a sense of community on the local level, where the communal life of the Church should be actually expressed and lived.

Let no-one, then, underestimate the significance and power of the liturgical movement. What is taking place is not the increasing popularity of a private hobby or interesting sideline, not a touching-up of ritual anomalies, but a change, a renewal in the pastoral work of the Church. And the concern is not with incidentals, but with the fundamentals of doctrine.